Designed by God so I must be Special

WRITTEN BY BONNIE SOSÉ

ILLUSTRATIONS BY BONNIE AND HOLLY SOSÉ

Copyright © 1988 Bonnie L. Sosé

By Character Builders for Kids
Aloma Business Center
6922 Aloma Avenue
Winter Park, FL 32792
407-677-7171
407-677-1010 FAX

This book is available through . . .
- Waldenbooks
- B-Dalton Booksellers
- Gift, Book & Childrens Speciality Stores

ISBN#0-9615279-6-X   White Version
ISBN#0-9615279-4-3   Afro-American Version

Dedicated To
All God's handcrafted gifts to life—
His Children

God gave me my eyes
so that I could see
all the beautiful things
around you and me;

Like turtles, and goldfish
and little bugs galore,
and when my very best friend,
comes knocking at my door.

There are butterflies of every color,
bunnies, frogs and puppies too,
rainbows, kittens and candy apples
just to name a few.

He gave me my ears
so that I could hear
all the many sounds
both far and near;

Like the Robin in her nest
who sings night and day
and when my mom says
"I love you" in her very special way.

There's that sweet lullaby
she sings to me each night
as she gently tucks me in bed
and turns out the light.

He gave me my nose
so that I could smell
all of grandma's goodies
and other things as well;

Like sugar-coated rainbow chunks
and marshmallow delight
or caramel candy popcorn
which is yummy to my bite.

And the smell of fresh baked pizza,
cookies, brownies and candies too.
What about the smell of red roses
He created for me and you?

He gave me my skin
so that I could feel,
all those great sensations
that are warm and real;

Like when my mom hugs me
and tickles my back
or when my little dog
jumps up into my lap.

There's that soak in the tub
after a cold rainy day,
and that squeeze from my dad
after he's been away.

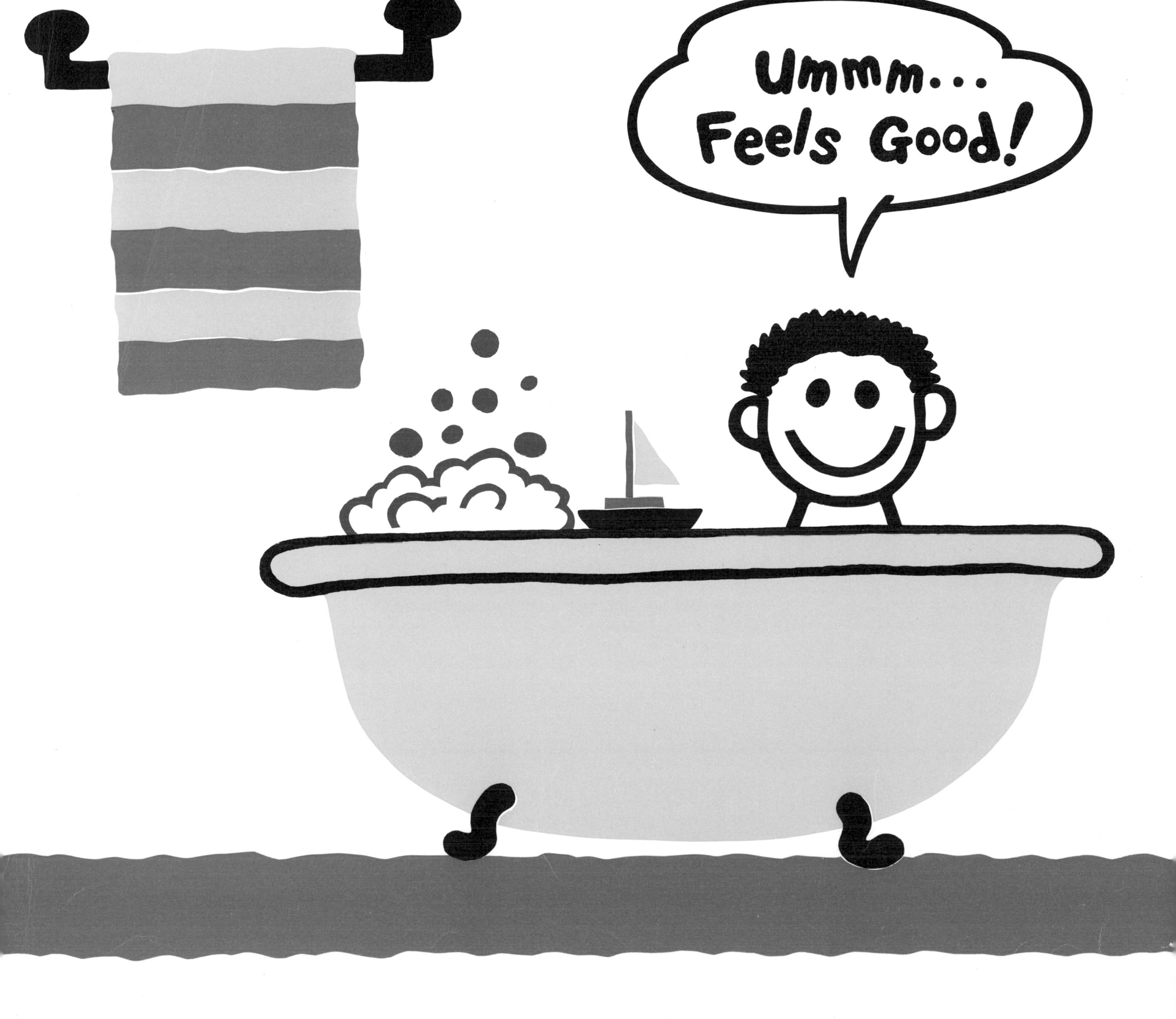
Ummm...
Feels Good!

He gave me my body
so that I could be free
to experience this world
around you and me;

Like jumping rope and running
and climbing big trees,
or playing freeze tag
and maybe looking for bees,

Also fishing and swimming
just to name a few,
and chasing my friends
both old and new.

He gave me my mind
so that I could dream
of lollipop castles
and moats of ice cream.

I can think and plan
and invent with my mind,
what a wonderful tool
I was so lucky to find.

I can imagine and dream.
Oh, what a great thrill!
I can go where I want
by the act of my will.

He gave me my heart
so I could feel
the many tender feelings
that **He** made so real;

Like the hurt in my heart
when a tiny bird falls from its nest,
and I pick him up gently
and tenderly give him my best,

Or that super-good feeling
when my aunt hugs me real tight,
then looks me in the eye
and smiles with delight.

He gave me my Spirit
so that I could know
that **He's** always beside me
every place that I go.

To love me, to protect me,
to show me the way,
to be there in hard times
as well as each day.

He designed me with Special talents,
gifts and abilities you see,
which let me know that **He** has
something **Special** in mind for me.

God made me Special!